Dating Chinese Wom[en]
Tips, Tricks & Techni[ques]

By Alex Coverdale

This work in its entirety is copyright of the author (2018). All rights reserved. No part of this work may be reproduced in any form without explicit written permission.

Contents

Introduction
The Basics
Initiating Contact
Making the First Move
Getting to know Each other
Sealing the Deal
Playing the Game
The Long Haul
Paying for It
Top Dating tips

Bonus Content:

This is China: Misadventures in the Middle Kingdom Part 1 – The North

Introduction

This book doesn't pull any punches. You'll find it full of real talk, actual situations and practical advice gleaned from many years of living in China, having Chinese friends, and dating almost exclusively Chinese women. It's not a tourist guide book, a travelogue, or a confessional. In a nutshell, this book is designed to help you date Chinese women.

You're probably thinking the answer to that question is, 'The same way as you'd date any other women.'

To an extent, you'd be right.

But you'd also be very wrong.

Because if you know anything at all about Chinese women, you'll know that there are no other species quite like them on earth. They are completely unique, and this calls for a different approach.

Perhaps the single greatest thing about Chinese women is the fact that, like other Asian women, most of them are crazy about foreigners. The simple reason for this is that they think everything Western is better than everything Chinese, including the men. Added to that, there is the inherent need to experience more than their conservative and often restrictive society allows them to, and forge a better life. In a culture where everyone is encouraged to behave and think the same way, they see foreigners as exciting, exhilarating and often intoxicating.

By some happy coincidence, to the average westerner Chinese women are also considered extremely desirable. Beautiful, submissive, and dutiful are three words commonly used to describe them. In most cases, you can add loyal, demure, intelligent, seductive and svelte to the list.

However, there is a preconception among both parties that the other is inaccessible. There aren't just geographical distances to overcome, but cultural, societal, and lingual ones, too. Metaphorically speaking, Western guys and Chinese women are worlds apart.

But it doesn't have to be that way.

There are around 700 million females in China alone. This figure doesn't even take into account women from the surrounding territories like Singapore and Taiwan, or ex-pats living further afield. There are over 9 million Chinese currently living in Thailand alone, and there are significant populations in Malaysia, Canada, Australia, France, the UK, the USA, and elsewhere in the world.

Obviously, not every one of these women will be identical. Despite what some people would have you believe, there is such a thing as individuality amongst the Chinese, and it's on the rise. The 'old' ways are quickly dying out. You may be surprised, however, at just how similar the majority of these women are, especially the ones still living in China. They shop in the same stores, listen to the same music, visit the same websites, learn from the same curriculum, and are encouraged at every turn to develop the same set of ideas and core values by the government-controlled media. They are, essentially, products of social conditioning, and consequently display many of the same character traits and mannerisms.

For that reason, there are certain assumptions and generalizations you can make with a higher than average level of confidence.

And that's where this book comes in.

It will teach you all you need to know about being with Chinese women at every step of a relationship. How to find them, how to approach them, how to get them into bed, how to form lasting partnerships with them, and perhaps most importantly, what they want from you.

I lived and worked in China for almost six years. I've had several serious long-term relationships with Chinese women, less-serious romantic dalliances with a bunch more, and even a few torrid one-night-stands and ill-advised romantic liaisons mixed in. To be brutally honest, I've lost count of the amount of Chinese women I've had sex with. If I was forced to put a figure on it, I would say the number is certainly in excess of 30, probably closer to 40, and maybe even 50 or more. That's not bad for a guy like me with average looks and an average income.

How did I do it?

Easy. I learned how to understand Chinese women, tell them what they want to hear, and treat them the way they want to be treated.

It was a long process full of trial and error, and it wasn't all plain-sailing. I've had good luck and bad, and faced my share of adversity. In fact, it's probably fair to say that I've encountered virtually every romantic situation it's possible to encounter, and that's even before everything is compounded by cultural clashes and language barriers.

Before I went to China, I had only ever dated British girls. I soon discovered that Chinese women are vastly different to everything I was accustomed to, and it took me a long time to get to the point where I was confident in dealing with them.

I picked up a lot of tricks and information along the way. Tricks and information which I am going to share with you. I set out to write the kind of book I wish I'd had access to when I first went to China, and I think I succeeded.

Wink.

The Basics

The obvious way to initially make contact with Chinese women is to go up and talk to them.

You just have to find them first.

Of course, you can try to meet them in your own country. But realistically and statistically, you'll have a far better chance if you actually get yourself to China. If you've never been, I urge you to seriously consider it.

Going there to work is a viable option. So is an extended holiday. According to World Atlas, China is the fourth most visited country in the world attracting 59.3 million tourists per year, behind only Spain, the USA and France. Full of unique sights, sounds and smells, going to China is truly a life-changing experience.

Depending on your country of origin, you will probably need to acquire a visa before you enter. The cost and application requirements vary, so check the Chinese embassy website in your country for details. You should be able to apply via post, or to accelerate the process you can go straight to the embassy and take the required documents and paperwork with you.

Try to avoid the organized tours and package deals. Despite what they might say, you'll have to pay no end of middlemen and facilitators, all of whom will want their cut. Just use https://www.skyscanner.net/ to find the cheapest available flight. It helps if you make your dates flexible. Then use https://www.booking.com to find a reasonably-priced hotel. Depending on the city, standard, and amenities, prices vary widely, but as a general guide you should be able to secure a three-star hotel in most major cities for less than 250 RMB (£28) per night, while an equivalent room in London would cost around £80 and New York £150 or more. Of course, if you are on a budget you can stay in lower standard accommodation like a traveller's hostel for a fraction of the price. It isn't difficult to find rooms in Beijing for £6 or £7 per night. Two other contributing factors are the time of year you travel, and how long in advance you book.

If you do decide on the holiday option, my advice would be to travel as much as possible, rather than spend all your time in one place. The infrastructure in China is generally good, so it's relatively cheap and easy to travel from city to city using the HSR (High Speed Rail, similar to Japanese bullet trains) or sleeper trains for longer distances. If, for argument's sake, you go for a month, you could comfortably accommodate six or more destinations.

Apart from taking a holiday to the Middle Kingdom, another option is to find a job there. It isn't that difficult. Most laowai (foreigners) go there to teach English, to satisfy the outrageous demand. If you are a native speaker, have a university degree (in any topic) and a clean criminal record, you won't have any problems finding gainful employment. A Teaching English as a Foreign Language (TEFL) or Teaching English as a Second Language (TESL) qualification is an advantage, as is being white. I know that sounds harsh, and in the modern age is morally repugnant, but it's the truth. Most foreign workers choose this option because it's so easy. Most jobs require you to fulfil as little as 14 or 16 teaching hours a week. The rest of the time is yours. People who are more serious about teaching can usually work their way up the ladder into management positions at state-run schools and universities, and especially training centres, quite quickly.

It's also possible to break into the lucrative International English Language Training System (IELTS) market. This is a test students who go to study abroad have to pass, and there's good money to be made as either an instructor or examiner. If you have aspirations of being a teacher in your own country, China is a good place to get experience, and looks great on your resume even if it isn't 'real' teaching. Things have gotten a little stricter in recent years following several widespread and much-needed government crackdowns, but English teaching is still a growth industry and represents your best chance of finding a job.

Of course, you don't HAVE to go into teaching. That's perhaps the easiest route, but there are unlimited options. In my time in China I rubbed shoulders with everyone from engineers and chemists to publicans and mineral traders. Just search for a job based on your qualifications, experience and skill-set. I won't waste any more time talking about that here. The best advice I can give is to do your research, work out what you want, and go for it. What have you got to lose?

Whatever path you choose, just do yourself a favour and keep your work life completely separate from your private life. It sounds simple, but you won't find it so easy to say 'no' when women are practically throwing themselves at you, which they probably will at some stage. I've been guilty of mixing business and pleasure myself in the past, and it never ends well. Relationships are difficult enough as it is, especially cross-cultural ones, without any added burden. You might be able to get away with a low-key fling or two, but anything else is asking for trouble.

That said, it's worth noting that the stigma about teachers dating their students we have in the West doesn't exist in China. Most of my colleagues have had illicit encounters with colleagues and/or students. At the risk of sounding cynical, be careful who you trust and always consider the WCS (Worst Case Scenario).

A friend of mine was teaching at a women's university in Hunan Province and bedded a couple of his students. He also had a habit of sexting them. Of course, girls talk, and a few of these girls got together and blackmailed him. They demanded cash, around 2000 RMB each, and 100% in their English exams, or they would tell the university Dean what had been going on.

Caught between a rock and a hard place, my friend complied. He gave them the cash, and the perfect scores. But the girls ratted him out anyway. He was called to the faculty office one morning and asked to explain himself. Naturally, he denied everything. Until the Dean produced printed copies of his cock and balls which he'd sent to the students and said, "So, this isn't yours?"

Not only was my friend sacked, but the school carried out an enquiry into his conduct, discovered some of the paperwork he'd been using was falsified, and had his work permit revoked. He was given a hefty fine, spent a couple of nights in a Chinese prison cell, and sent home in disgrace. The last I heard, he was working in a supermarket in Norwich. Learn from his mistakes. The old adage 'don't shit where you eat' most definitely applies.

Some places write awfully tacky terms like 'intercourse with students strictly forbidden' into their contracts, not that contracts mean much in China. In my opinion there's nothing wrong with dating your students, providing they are old enough, obviously, and you don't create a conflict of interest. As one of my colleagues was fond of reiterating, being attracted to beautiful 21-year old girls is the most natural thing in the world. Just be smart about it. Be discreet, and avoid drawing unnecessary attention to yourselves.

After a couple of years, I developed a strategy of working at a university for a semester or two before moving to a different one.

Then, all bets are off and as consenting adults you can do whatever you want. I made sure I stayed in touch with all the hot girls, and must have bedded a dozen or more using this simple method.

As for locations, you will find more opportunities and higher salaries in the booming metropolises like Beijing, Shanghai, Guangzhou and Shenzhen, but the cost of living is higher and the pace of life is faster. There is also more competition for jobs. My preference is for slightly smaller cities, which have a good infrastructure but are less chaotic. There are literally hundreds. China has 14 cities of over 5 million, while the USA has eight and India seven.

Amusingly, there is an annual 'Happiest City in China' ranking, which might help you make a decision. It started in Oriental Outlook magazine, but was then picked up by the national and then world media. They take into account things like the environment, job satisfaction, living standards, public services, security, and numerous other factors. At the time of writing, the most recent city to be crowned 'Happiest in China' was Chengdu in Sichuan province. Making up the rest of the top ten were Hangzhou, Ningbo, Nanjing, Changchun, Xi'an, Changsha, Taizhou, Tongchuan and Xuzhou.

When you make your decision, bear in mind the Great Heating Divide, the imaginary line that roughly dissects China along the Huai River and Qin mountains. To the north of the line there is central heating in the winter (switched on and controlled by the government), and to the south there isn't. Central heating is one of the luxuries we often take for granted in the West. It gets warmer the further south you go but believe me, being on the wrong side of that line during winter isn't much fun. In places like Harbin, Jinan and Tianjin in the far north, winter temperatures regularly drop well below -36 degrees.

Another factor to consider, believe it or not, is the physical characteristics of the women. In the north, they tend to be taller, thicker-set and with more angled features while in the south they are generally smaller, slimmer, cuter and have darker skin. A lot of people say southern Chinese women look more south-east Asian (Thai, Vietnamese, Filipino) while their northern counterparts are considered more north-east Asian (Japanese, Mongol, Korean, etc).

Despite their generally better looks, southern Chinese women also have a reputation for being more fiery and money-oriented, while northern women tend to be more caring and domesticated. I spent my first two years in northern China, in Beijing and Tianjin to be precise, and a common saying among Chinese guys in those regions was, "In south China the food is hot, and the women are hotter."

Only after moving there did I come to realize that they meant 'hotter' as in bad-tempered, rather than better looking!

There are recognisable differences between north and south. As with most things, it boils down to a simple matter of taste. Try both, and see which you like best.

The Chinese have a very fixed idea of beauty, and it differs somewhat from the western ideal. This can be confusing at times, because women we see as drop-dead gorgeous may not even turn the head of a Chinese guy. This, obviously, is an advantage for non-Chinese who have altogether different standards. For starters, while western girls spend small fortunes on tanning, in China they value pale skin. Supermarkets and drug stores are full of whitening creams and lotions. This is because in ancient times, dark skin was associated with poverty. Added to this they favour long legs, slim figures, full lips, big eyes, high cheekbones and a small nose. An increasing number of women resort to cosmetic surgery to 'enhance' their beauty, one of the most common procedures being a blepharoplasty to create a double eye-lid. This has the dual purpose of making the eyes look bigger, and more Western.

Conversely, several cities in China claim to have the most desirable women. Yangzhou, a small city in Jiangsu province, has been known as the 'birthplace of beauties' since ancient times. In truth, there are more than several. Suzhou, Chengdu, Xi'an, Datong, Dalian, Wuhan, Chongqing, Anqing, and Nanjing, make similar claims. Don't worry, to help you get to the bottom of it, there was a recent study on the website www.china.org.cn similar to that carried out to determine the 'Happiest City in China' which put Harbin in top spot saying, "The girls there are probably the tallest in China. Walking on the street will make you feel like you are watching a cat-walk."

The downside is that Harbin is one of the coldest places on earth so you know, swings and roundabouts.

Making Contact

Okay, so you now have a new job or a holiday planned, somewhere to stay, and you know where the most beautiful (or at least, tallest) women are. Let's crack on with your love life. Before you go, you need to start social networking. I am assuming you have a smartphone, or at least access to a computer. There are lots of websites and dating apps designed to help you along, most charging a fee. The biggest and most popular right now are probably www.asiandating.com and www.asiacharm.com but a quick Google search using terms like 'Chinese partner' will yield many more results. Don't just sign up and pay the membership fees on a whim, do some research, read the reviews, and make an informed decision.

I know numerous people who've had success with these sites and others like them, but in my experience, the best two to use are free. https://www.wechat.com/en/ is a chat app, available for Apple or Android. Think of it as a Chinese Facebook. People post updates, pictures, and news links, but the main purpose is to communicate with people in your circle.

By the way, using actual Facebook can be problematic because it is banned in China, along with YouTube, Twitter, Hotmail, most blogging sites and even some foreign news sites. That isn't to say you can't use these platforms in China. The restrictions on internet use are easily circumnavigated by using a VPN. There are lots available, some free, some paid for. As a rule, the paid-for variety are generally more reliable. I recommend https://www.expressvpn.com which offers a free trial. Remember to install the VPN before you go because most of the VPN sites themselves are blocked. Crafty.

Not only does WeChat help keep all your contacts in one place, but you can use the built-in 'people nearby' facility to meet new ones. Seeking out and joining groups in WeChat is also a good way to meet women. One of the most useful functions in is the Chinese-English translator, which enables you to communicate with people who don't speak a word of English. Be warned, the translator isn't always 100% accurate, but it usually does the job.

The other free app I recommend is Tantan (https://tantanapp.com/en/), a dating app, often known as a Chinese Tinder. It's easy to use. You set distance parameters, then swipe left on the photos you don't like and right on the photos you do.

Obviously, the more you swipe right the more chance you have of matching with someone. This app has a reputation for being the one people use to find sex, rather than something people use to find long-term relationships.

Alternatives are Momo and Let's Have Dinner, both of which readily available from the App Store. Another social networking site called QQ also still has a lot of users, but is rapidly going out of fashion. Think of that one as like a Chinese MySpace. An increasing number of Chinese singles also use Tinder and Plenty of Fish, so to increase your chances double (or triple) up and use more than one.

Don't wait until after you arrive. Download a couple of these apps and get started right now. I didn't start using Tantan until after I went back to the UK, where it proved extremely useful in locating Chinese women in my local area. After only a couple of weeks I was dating a university student from Dalian, and for the rest of her stay in the UK we would meet for no-strings sex in cities all over the country. I would never have met her had it not been for Tantan. The trick is to be open and honest about what you want. Though not too open and honest (see next chapter). If you are using Tantan, the odds are the women you talk to know what you are after, anyway.

Use these channels correctly and you can line up a string of dates before you even arrive in China.

As with all online activity, however, exercise a bit of caution. If something seems too good to be true, it probably is. I've encountered several gay guys posing as hot women, complete with fake pictures. The giveaway is that they usually ask you for dick pics almost instantly. Genuine women, especially Asian women, are very rarely that forward. If I'm suspicious, I simply ask them to send me a voice message. A feminine voice is harder to fake.

There's also a popular phishing scam you should be aware of, variations of which happen on most online platforms. A hot woman sends you a friend request, starts chatting, and in no time at all gets flirty and engages you in a sexually-charged conversation. She asks you for intimate photos, or instigates a video call, then encourages you to perform solo sex acts for her, while she does the same. If you do, ahem, pleasure yourself for the camera, she will record it and threaten to share the video online unless you pay her an extortionate amount of money.

Don't.

If you ever find yourself in such a compromising position, just block her and forget about it.

As a final tip, stock up on chocolate before you leave and take it with you. You can get Snickers, Dove, and one or two other brands in China but generally, good-quality chocolate is extremely hard to find and is worth its weight in gold. Women go crazy for it, not least because to them it represents wealth and status.

As you will have noted by now, meeting women in China isn't difficult. However, breaking through those social constraints, the language barrier, and overcoming the myriad cultural differences, often is. I'm going to talk about Chinese women in a general sense, based on my own experiences and those of my friends and colleagues. What follows in subsequent chapters are meant to be guidelines and anecdotes highlighting potential problems and offering solutions as to how to overcome them. The conclusions are by no means meant to apply to every single woman in the country. I am sure you are aware, in the dating game there are very few hard and fast rules. And even if there were, there would always be exceptions. This isn't a book for or about pick-up artists. That's a whole different area. If that's what you're looking for, I recommend The Game by Neil Strauss. It will teach you hundreds of tricks and techniques which you can use to your heart's content. Some of these techniques might even work on Asian girls.

Dating Asian women, specifically Chinese women, is the same sport, but a different league. This means you can't go about your business in quite the same way. But as I alluded to before, when you've learned how to unlock it, you can open the door to a whole world of possibilities.

The First Move

One of the preconceptions about Chinese women is that they are shy and reserved. This assumption is generally accurate, at least outwardly. To Chinese people in general, public image is exceptionally important. They call it 'face.' In pin yin (the anglicized version of Mandarin/Cantonese) it is called 'mian zi' and it doesn't refer to the physical representation. It's more of an image thing. To them, 'losing face,' or being embarrassed in public, is like the worst thing in the world.

Because of this prevailing shyness, you will probably find that the vast majority are much happier to talk online than they are in person, at least in the early stages. Part of this is the fact that they are not very confident in their English and wary of communication difficulties. There are also a lot of perverts online who jump in with the dick pics and dirty talk far too soon. Don't be THAT guy. By all means, that stuff is fine later on, when your relationship reaches that level, but don't force the issue. Chinese women are generally not very receptive to sexually aggressive behaviour by virtual strangers.

That said, in Chinese culture, the onus is very much on the man to take control of the situation and make the running, so you have to strike a balance.

I usually try to exonerate myself by offering a 'pre-emptive apology.' I will explain that Western culture is much more open than Chinese culture and while I respect it very much, I am not exactly sure where 'the line' is and I am sorry in advance if I ever cross it. This little prepared speech achieves many things. Firstly, it reinforces what the girl thinks she already knows. Secondly, it paints me as a caring, conscientious guy who is concerned about her feelings. And thirdly, it raises the whole topic of 'openness' and makes it clear you are comfortable talking about it. It plants the seed.

If a girl likes you, she will usually let it be known in subtle ways like saying 'goodnight' before she goes to sleep or checking on your well-being. But in general, they can often appear cold and stand-offish, especially at first. Keep the opening exchanges simple and be polite. Stick to safe bets like "Hi, nice to meet you!" and ask a lot of questions about her likes and dislikes, her home town, China in general, music, movies, travel. I always say there is one topic all Chinese women absolutely love talking about, and that's food. Food is so intrinsically important to the Chinese that they can quite happily talk about it for months on end. Avoid potentially hazardous topics like politics and religion.

An easy ice-breaker is to express an interest in learning Chinese and offer to teach them English in return for Chinese lesson. This means you can get to know each other without the added pressure of 'dating' or being in an actual relationship. When I first moved to China in 2007, I soon learned that being 'language partners' was an accepted euphemism for someone you are kinda interested in. Looking at it from a practical perspective, when there are so many prospective language partners, why would you choose one you weren't attracted to, anyway?

In real life, there are the obvious places to meet the opposite sex like bars and clubs. Most of the larger cities have an abundance of these. Statistically, you would stand a higher than average chance of hooking up in one of these places simply because the kind of women who frequent them are often just looking for excitement and some no-strings fun. According to many of my Chinese friends, there is a general feeling amongst women that they look for foreigners for fun, and Chinese guys for something more serious, which usually results in marriage. The average age of marriage in China is a lot lower than in the West. For example, current figures stand at 23 for women and 25 for men in China compared with 30 and 32 in the UK.

The very first sex I had in China was a one night stand with someone I met in a club. I was getting myself a drink at the bar and a woman next to me said, "Let me get that for you." An hour later, we were back at her place. I wish I could remember more about it, but I was pretty drunk. It happens. Being foreign means you stand out, and some women are attracted to the 'free' lifestyle they think we enjoy. For this reason, women of a certain persuasion flock to ex-pat bars, which are increasing in China. Some are even run by foreigners. You'll find them in most cities. Become a regular, spend a bit of money, and get to know the owners and clientele.

It's not just older women who go to bars and clubs looking for 'fun' with Western guys. I know several 19 and 20-year old's who frequent them and regularly pick up one-night stands. This used to be exceptionally rare, promiscuity is frowned upon in China, but it's becoming more and more prevalent in modern society. Incidentally, these same 19 and 20-year old girls are on Tantan and Tinder.

You might come across bar girls in China, especially in the more liberal cities like Hong Kong and Guangzhou. These usually operate in the same way as the more familiar bar girls in Thailand and elsewhere in Asia. They are employed by the bar, and their job is to simply keep patrons company and make sure they have a good time. Of course, if they can get them to part with sizeable amounts of cash it's a bonus.

The girls have various little tricks they employ. One thing they do is get you to order a round of shots for the table, telling you she'll get you a good deal. To start with, even with a discount, shots are expensive wherever you go. But to rub salt in the wound, she will make sure that her 'shot' is a shot of water. The establishment, however, will charge you for an extra shot of tequila or whatever.

Alternatively, the girl might ask you to buy her a cocktail. You'll certainly be charged for one, but what the girl will actually get will be a soft drink or glass of fruit juice made to look like a cocktail. Bar girls might have the occasional alcoholic drink, but they don't want to be wasted on the job. And the bars that hire them wouldn't allow it, anyway. If they can pull this trick off a few times a night (good bar girls will be able to pull it off a few times an hour) it can be an excellent money-spinner.

When it comes to taking these girls home, it's their prerogative. The premises won't endorse such behaviour because they don't want to get in trouble with the authorities, but they turn a blind eye to what the girls do. Consenting adults and all that. It's really not much different than going out and having a one night stand. These girls tend to be more picky than run-of-the-mill prostitutes, and they will generally only go home with guys they like. If she is into you, she will let you know sooner rather than later. Then you discuss a price and either come to an agreement, or if you aren't interested she moves on to the next mark. Sometimes, you are also expected to pay a fee to the house to take the girl outside. Lots of Western guys favour this way of 'meeting' girls. Keep in mind, however, that by the time you pay for a couple of overpriced fake cocktails, the house fee, the girl's fee, plus maybe a cab and a bite to eat, it can get a little expensive. For more on this topic, please see the chapter entitled, 'Paying for it.'

If going to bars and clubs isn't your thing, don't worry about it. You will also find an abundance of single ladies in shopping malls, cafes, supermarkets, parks, museums, libraries and public attractions of all descriptions.

Chinese women have pre-conceived ideas of what a 'gentleman' is, and it's easy to play up to that. Introduce yourself and pretend to be lost, or ask for directions. A nice trick is to ask her opinion on something. This gives the impression that you value her thoughts and ideas. You can expect to be rejected a lot, obviously. But this is a numbers game, so the more women you approach the higher your chances become. It's like being a footballer. The more shots you attempt, the more goals you score.

Approach them in much the same way you would a western girl, but with one crucial difference. You don't need any fancy openers here. You're foreign, so she is already interested in what you have to say. Just be non-threatening, smile a lot, and over polite. Preface whatever you say with, "Excuse me, miss. Do you speak any English?" The vast majority speak at least some, but you are also giving her a convenient 'get out' clause. If she isn't interested she can just say "no" and you can both move on.

Taking part in extra-curricular activities is another good way to meet women. Join a gym, a social club, or a Chinese class and look out for cultural events and activities like dumpling making and tea ceremony classes. Chinese women are very proud of their culture and history, and would love to tell you more about it. Also, the male-female ratio at most of these events is heavily weighted in your favour. Bonus.

If that's too much trouble, volunteer for English corners or English clubs. You won't have to spend too long looking for them. As soon as the people who run them find out there is a new foreigner in town, they'll be begging you to get involved. Many private schools run such events to attract new students, and it isn't unheard of for teachers at different places to swap duties and appear at each other's English corners just to meet new women.

Don't be surprised if girls come up to you and ask for your phone number. Guys do it, too. That's a little disconcerting, but is a product of the general kudos that comes with having foreign 'friends,' especially in the smaller towns and cities where it's more of a novelty. Take it in your stride and don't get too excited. The phone number thing can lead to all kinds of misunderstandings. In Western culture, if a girl comes up and asks for your number, or even better, gives you hers, you could be forgiven for thinking you'd be onto a winner. Otherwise, she wouldn't give you her number, right?

Wrong. It's not that simple in China. Most things aren't that simple in China. There are huge cultural differences.

Let's, for example, say that you are out walking one afternoon, meet a woman, make a bit of small talk and exchange phone or WeChat numbers. You might go home and send her a message. The odds are, she won't reply.

Yeah, she might be busy, so you leave it a day or two and text her again.

No reply.

If she is especially hot, or you are especially desperate, you might try one more time.

Still no reply.

It's at this point that most Western guys give up, because in our culture if a girl doesn't reply to your messages she isn't interested.

Not necessarily so in China.

There, they value patience and persistence much more than western girls do. If you ask Chinese couples to tell you how they met, it's not unusual to hear slightly creepy tales of overly possessive behaviour and what, to our Western minds, sound a lot like stalking. One girl I know told me that her then-boyfriend won her over by standing outside her dormitory every night and following her whenever she went out. In the end, she just gave in and 'accepted' his love, whereas most Western women probably would have called the police.

What does this all mean?

It means that if you stop texting that girl after only one or two unanswered messages, she will think you didn't really like her much anyway. Because if you did like her that much, you wouldn't have given up so easily.

Get it?

The longer you pursue her without reward, or to put it another way, the more you bombard her with unreciprocated attention, the more she will think you like her because it's much easier to just give up and focus your attention elsewhere.

She might even go one better and tell you flat out that she isn't interested. That happened to me several times. Don't believe it.

Unless you've made a massive fool of yourself somehow, if she wasn't interested she wouldn't have given you her phone number in the first place, and she certainly wouldn't waste her time talking to you. She's testing your resolve. The last girl to tell me she just wanted to be 'friends' was sending me naked photos hours later.

You can forget the usual Western dating paradigm altogether. Normal rules do not apply with Chinese women. To lessen the pressure on her, instead of asking her out on a bona fide date, try starting things off slowly by inviting her on a couple of mini-dates. Suggest meeting for a cup of coffee one morning, or better still, turn up near where she works one afternoon, say you just happened to be in the area, and take her out for lunch.

Where possible, build things up slowly. More than likely, she has more than one suitor and your first job will be to make a good impression and stand out from the crowd. I was on a date once with a woman from Shanghai. I was having fun, and feeling a bit cocky, so at one point, with my tongue firmly in cheek, I asked her where she'd been all my life. She looked at me and without missing a beat, and with no trace of humour or irony, said, "Dating other guys."

Yeah, so women often approach you in the street. Some will say they want to practise English with you, and most are genuine. We've been through that. But there's a popular scam you should be aware of here. Scammers operate all over Asia. Indeed, the world. If you're lucky, you will never encounter any. But if one day you are walking down a street and are approached by a couple of cute, smiling, enthusiastic young Chinese ladies who suggest taking you somewhere to 'practise English,' be suspicious. What they sometimes do is take you to a local tea shop or similar establishment, order drinks, then after a while 'get a phone call' and leave suddenly sticking you with the bill.

Under normal circumstances, this wouldn't be a problem, beverages are generally quite reasonable in China. But this tea shop is in on the act, and presents you with an extortionate bill amounting to thousands of yuan (equivalent to hundreds of pounds). If you refuse to pay, the owners and staff intimidate you and threaten to call the police. If and when the police DO come, the chances are they will side with the tea shop anyway, either because they are on the take, or because the proprietor can point out what you had, and then show the police a (fake) menu listing comparable prices.

If you ever find yourself in such a predicament, the solution is simple. Don't stick around arguing and causing a scene. Run. That's exactly what a friend of mine did when this happened to him in Guangzhou.

If and when you succeed in setting up a date, bear in mind that you'll be expected to pay for everything. It's increasingly common in the West for couples to 'go Dutch.' Known in the Middle Kingdom as 'AA.'

Not in China. Here, the man assumes the role of provider while the woman will show her affection and appreciation by taking on a more nurturing role. She might cook you meals or tell you to go to bed early because it's 'good for your body.' Interesting point here; the Chinese think water is some kind of wonder drug, and you'll often be told to 'drink more water' for no apparent reason. Just go with it.

Getting to know Each other

Let's be honest here. When I talk about 'dating' what I am really talking about is sex. Or, more specifically, mastering the skills of seduction. As I've said before, and will continue to do so throughout this book to emphasis its importance, the key is not to rush things. If you are on the dating scene in China and not committed to any one woman, you will probably end up nurturing several relationships at the same time, which will all moving at different paces and be at various stages of development. I spent almost six years there, and apart from a barren first six months or so when I was finding my feet, I was meeting women continuously. I kept lots of irons in the fire, and in the couple of weeks before I left I pulled all those irons out and slept with a different woman every day. Sometimes two. That's not even an exaggeration.

In some cases it was 'goodbye sex,' with old flames. Other times, it was kind of 'Well, if we don't do it now, we never will.' It might sound like a dream come true. But trust me, it's both physically and emotionally exhausting.

Chinese women appreciate a man who is controlled, confident and assertive, especially when it comes to decision-making. They want someone to take the lead. It makes their whole lives easier. Other qualities they look for are kindness, generosity and empathy.

If you want to make a good impression, play the role of gentleman. Open doors for her, pull out the chair before she sits down, be attentive and charming. Compliment her on everything. Not just the obvious like her hair or dress, let her know you are noticing the small things. Earrings, nails, eyes, nose, and more nuanced aspects like her disposition and sense of humour. Beautiful women know they are beautiful and get tired of hearing the same shit over and over again.

Don't be surprised if, on your first date, or first couple of dates, the object of your affection turns up with a friend or two in tow. I think they do it for moral support. Treat these girls (sometimes boys) like gold. Buy them dinner, practise English with them, cater to their whims. Make allies of them. It's all about making a good impression so they say good things about you. In essence, it's playground stuff. If you win over the friends, it will be a million times easier to win over the object of your affection.

A quick word here on the male/female social dynamic. You will hear a lot of girls referring to their 'brothers.' In most cases, due to the one-child policy, these guys are not brothers at all but cousins, other relations, neighbours, or even just close friends. Sometimes they represent your competition, so be wary of that. By assuming the role of 'fake brother' they often fly under the radar.

For their part, Chinese guys like having attractive girls (sisters) around because it makes them look good in front of their peers. The girls are very often just there for show, and they know it. Most of their guy friends won't even interact with them, unless they are drunk in KTV. If you can engage with them and make her feel you can see beyond her looks, it will pay off later.

When you first start dating, it's not unusual for a woman to ask you very intimate and direct questions about how much money you have. She will want to know details about your salary, your earning power, your assets, your savings. To westerners, this can appear a bit mercenary, if not downright rude. The flip-side is that in many ways, Chinese women are actually less superficial in the sense that they don't care so much about looks. They care about money and material possessions more, and make no bones about it.

They want to be looked after.

To understand why, you need a handle on the social backdrop in China. The bottom line is everyone wants a better life, and in the absence of state pensions, health insurance policies, the NHS, and other such safety nets, access to money takes on added importance, especially when planning for the future. Until comparatively recently, China was virtually a third world country, and many of the practices forged in those dark times persist.

China isn't as poverty-stricken as it once was, but the rise of the middle and upper classes makes people look enviously at their neighbours. Everyone wants what everyone else has, and if they can't have it they want to know why. When discussing your finances, explain yourself adequately and present a sound logic, preferably along with a plan of action, or she might very well find someone who *can* give her those things. That said, it's okay to be vague about certain matters. For example, I always stress that I have 'investments' without going into too much detail.

Meeting the parents is an experience. I've met three or four sets of Chinese parents and, despite the language barrier, most were nice enough. At least, they were to my face. Learn a few words of Chinese for them, so they can see you are making an effort, and be extra-attentive and ultra-respectful with regards to their daughter. They want to see that you are completely and utterly devoted.

It can be disconcerting, however. I went on a date with a girl in Tianjin once, and she brought her dad along. Awkward. After dinner, the three of us went back to my apartment where 'Baba' watched TV while I took his daughter in the bedroom to listen to music. The door remained open. Frankly, I wasn't disappointed with that. I can't think of anything more weird than having sex with a girl when her father is in the next room, probably listening.

Another time, the girl's mother insisted on me taking the entire extended family out for dinner. They chose a top-end place and selected every expensive dish on the menu; crayfish, shark-fin soup, roasted duck. The meal ended up costing me almost half a month's salary.

You will find in China that when it comes to settling a bill, most of the guys in the group stand up, flash wads of cash around, and make a big song and dance about offering to pay. Most of them have no real intention of paying, they are just showing off. Not that time. When the waitress brought the bill, every other guy in the place sank sheepishly in their seats and pretended not to see her.

If that wasn't enough, after the meal I was coerced into taking the girl and her mother shopping, which put a significant dent in the rest of my wage packet. After buying my girlfriend a new coat, we went to about a dozen shops looking for a pair of shoes for mum. She couldn't find any she liked. Not what you need after a full day's teaching. In retrospect, the whole thing was like an elaborate character test to see if I was worthy of dating her daughter. The entire exercise turned out to be academic when I found out the girl had been cheating on me with a Romanian chef all along.

Gifts are good, and appreciated. Clothes, accessories, electronics, flowers. You have to give her things she doesn't have. It becomes almost like a form of prostitution sometimes. You give the girl what she wants, and she gives you what you want.

Don't let it get out of hand. I've heard of guys buying women cars, apartments, and handing over huge lump sums for 'business deals.' The golden rule here is to retain control. Generally, the more you give her, the more she will want. Be firm and learn to say 'no,' or she will bleed you dry. And when she's done, she'll move on to the next mark without giving you a second glance.

Make no bones about it. For all their good points, Chinese women can be extremely ruthless, not to mention manipulative. That is an observation, not a slur.

While on a trip to Shanghai, I met a girl called Jody and we struck up what can best be described as a close friendship. When I moved to Changsha in Hunan province, she suggested coming to stay with me for a week. Of course, I readily agreed. We weren't yet sleeping together and not wanting to rush things, I let her stay in the spare bedroom. The week visit turned into two weeks, then three, then four. We did have sex once. If you can call it that. One night, my bedroom door opened and she came in. Without a word, she kissed me, and eased herself onto my dick. She rode me until she came, which she did almost immediately. Then, she got up and left, telling me I could 'finish' myself.

Weird.

Our relationship wasn't progressing as I'd hoped, and it slowly began to dawn on me that rather than a girlfriend, I had a lodger who didn't contribute anything toward the upkeep of the apartment. This notion was reinforced when one day I came home from work and found her sister had also come to stay 'for a few days or so.'

I let them stay another week, until I heard them discussing having 'an aunt' over to stay as well. Like 'brother,' in China the word 'aunt' could mean almost anybody. Even if she was a genuine aunt, the apartment wasn't big enough for all four of us. Coincidentally, around this time, Jody left a chat window open on the apartment's computer (it belonged to my school) and went out. She was talking to a Chinese guy. Obviously, I used an online translator to see what they were talking about. She told him "Yes, your little bird flew away. But she will fly back again soon."

It didn't take much brain power to work out she was talking to her boyfriend. I didn't know she had a boyfriend. I just assumed that if she did, she would tell me. Wrong. That was when I had a quiet word and got rid of her and her sister.

Be wary of falling into the 'Chinese dating' trap, whereby guys try to win girls over by constantly doing them favours and buying them things. If you're foreign, the chances are, one of the reasons she is attracted to you is because you represent an adventurous, exotic option. You can break convention, and get away with a lot more than a Chinese guy would. If she pulls you up on any perceived sleight, just claim ignorance. Remember, though, that generosity is a highly-valued quality and nobody likes a tight ass.

The Chinese in general have a tendency to over-analyse. Any romantic partner you have will analyse you, herself, your relationship, your background, your career, your motivations, and pretty much everything else. As I just alluded to, Chinese women are also notorious for setting romantic partners a succession of tests, which you are expected to pass with flying colours if she is ever going to consider getting into a serious relationship with you. She will spend your money, instigate arguments, or perhaps criticize you, your friends, your habits or your country. I once had to patiently explain to a woman that neither I, nor any of my direct ancestors, had any involvement in the Opium Wars.

How you react to these tests, which are designed to assess your character and temperament, will determine whether or not you meet the criteria. If you fail, she won't think twice about deleting your number and social media, and completely shutting you out of her life. As a general rule, don't lose your temper, especially in public. Take whatever she says with a pinch of salt.

The most problematic consequence of the one-child policy is the gender imbalance. The fact that most families wanted sons for their increased earning power and the resultant willingness to abort female foetuses, has resulted in over 33 million more men than women in China.

Another weighty issue is the pressure piled on children to provide for their parents and grandparents when they get older and stop working. Chinese people naturally tend to be more filial and family-oriented, but the 4-2-1 problem, when the solitary child (1) is expected to look after his or her parents (2), as well as both sets of grandparents (4), on a single salary, is well documented. Obviously, this problem is exacerbated when two products of the one-child policy get together creating an 8-4-2 situation, and even more so when they try to start their own family and have even more mouths to feed.

The one-child policy has led to other interesting developments. A lot of people in China, especially when they are children, are afflicted by what has become known as 'Little Emperor' syndrome. Being the only offspring, they are spoiled and doted on by relatives, which sometimes creates a selfish, spiteful and self-centred personality. This is completely at odds with the many of the government-promoted 'we're all in this together' ideals and causes obvious problems when they are expected to fit into a society. The one-child policy, which has been called the biggest social experiment in history, has now been relaxed, but it will take many generations for the effects to wear off and balance out.

None of this means that women won't sleep with you if you're poor. She might. It's all relative. There will always be someone better off, and someone worse off than you. But she probably won't respect you quite as much as she would if you were wedged up, and won't be as committed. Money talks. That's why you see fat, old, ugly (usually married) Chinese businessmen cavorting around with hot young things half their age or younger.

Believe me, this thought process isn't that far removed from that of western women. Number one on most women's list, regardless of where they come from, is 'security.' It's just that Chinese women are more direct about it and won't try to spare your feelings. It's up to you what you tell them when they ask about your financial situation. But as I said, it wouldn't be unheard of to stretch the truth just a little to enhance your chances. Most Chinese (and Asian people in general) automatically assume when they meet foreigners, especially white guys, that they have money. Another preconception is that we are better endowed than our Asian counterparts. Whether that's true or not, it's sometimes advantageous to live up to the 'bigger wallets and bigger dicks' stereotype and let people think what they want to think.

Incidentally, if you are lucky enough to meet a rich Chinese woman, you will probably find she is single and desperate for affection. This is because, unlike western men, the majority of Chinese guys would be intimidated and even embarrassed if they were dating a woman who had more money than they did.

You may find Chinese people to be very direct and abrupt in other ways, too. For example, don't be surprised if someone walks up to you and calls you fat, even if you're not, or says you have a big nose, even if you don't. This is partly a result of having a limited English vocabulary, but in both cases it goes slightly deeper than that. Being fat is not seen as a negative in China. Remember that not so long ago, the country was poverty-stricken and it's people starving in the streets. To be even slightly overweight meant you were rich.

Regarding the second 'insult,' it's an antiquated term, and in the modern day can sometimes be interpreted as derisory, but an old Chinese name for foreigners is 'Big nose.' In some quarters, Big Nose is a kind of slang term, and not considered a personal insult.

Social proof is another big turn-on for Chinese women. Be popular. Even if you're Bobby Ordinary in your real life, in China you can be whatever or whoever you want. Reinvent yourself. Dress up occasionally when you go out, and wear some nice aftershave or cologne. I can't stress this too much. Not many Chinese guys bother, and it will really set you apart from the crowd. The same goes for personal and dental hygiene, believe it or not.

Incidentally, the same sometimes applies to women. They rarely wear perfume or shave their armpits, and bad breath is a recurring problem. It's best to just tell her you'd like her more if she brushed her teeth regularly. I was seeing a girl from a rural area of Hunan province. One evening over dinner she asked me if we were officially dating. I replied in the affirmative. She said, in all seriousness, "Does this mean I have to wash every day now?"

Yes. Yes it does.

Sealing the Deal

You will generally find women in China less sexually open than Western women. Some of the more westernised have similar attitudes to us, especially the Tinder generation, but often, the sex issue is an absolute minefield. One wrong move, and you'll blow yourself up.

Traditionally, a girl's virginity is highly prized, and if you are her first, that's serious. In fact, if you have sex with any Chinese women, they generally take it more seriously than Western women do. Even if you are a bit of fun, or a one-night stand, it means something to them. By the same token, lots of Chinese guys won't even consider going out with a woman who isn't a virgin.

What effect does this have?

Well, firstly, it increases the already-crippling levels of shame, anxiety and embarrassment Chinese women attach to sex. Secondly, it turns most of them into liars. The majority will sleep with guys who, being guys, pile on the pressure, and then just lie about it afterwards.

I used to date a girl called Skye (girls will assume English names, or at least English-sounding names, because most foreigners can't pronounce their Chinese names correctly. The weirdest 'name' I ever came across was a girl called Lube). Skye was 24, and still a virgin. It wasn't because she was ugly. On the contrary, she was extremely beautiful. But she was a 'traditional' girl who didn't want to have sex until after she got married. I did manage to finger her once, and it made her cry. Not cute little sniffles, she was howling. After that, I felt bad and ended our relationship. I soon found someone more open-minded.

Another time, I went on a date with a girl called Cherry (I shit you not). To cut a long story short, we ended up in bed together and it was then that I found out she'd never had sex, or even been touched before. I wasn't very serious about her, so not wanting to be the kind of guy who took the most precious thing she had to give then ran off, I excused myself and went to the pub, thinking she would be gone when I got back.

She wasn't, so I slept on the sofa. I thought I was doing the gentlemanly thing, but the next day Cherry was angry and said my perceived rejection her was the most humiliating thing to ever happen to her. She never forgave me. That obsession with 'face' again. In situations like that, good guys really do finish last. I should have just fucked her.

That reminds me of another time I was in bed with a woman and just about to slip it in. She had a momentary freak out and said she didn't want to do it, so I turned over and went to sleep. The next day she asked me why I stopped.

"Because you said 'no?'" I replied.

"Yeah," she said. "But I didn't mean it."

"But where I come from, if you say 'no' and I do that anyway, that's rape and I'm going to jail."

"Oh. Well, sometimes Chinese girls don't mean everything they say."

That was another valuable lesson. Apparently, she had been trying to protect her modesty and again, by not 'forcing' her, I had inadvertently paid her massive disrespect.

Complicated.

I told her in no uncertain terms that the next time I saw her, I wouldn't be such a gentleman. She came over that very night.

I've said before that Chinese girls like to foster that innocent, demure image. Some of the more traditional girls genuinely are innocent. This isn't just a result of the often oppressive society, but sex in general is still considered a very taboo topic. There is minimal, if any, sex education in schools, and the subject is often avoided at all costs even amongst close friends. Parents certainly never tell their offspring about the birds and the bees. Several times, girls I've been with have had orgasms and not known what was happening to them. One legitimately thought she was having a heart attack.

This general ignorance about sexual matters affects both sexes in China, meaning that western partners have a reputation for being better in bed simply on the basis of coming from a more open culture and having more life experience.

Most Chinese people don't even talk about sex, and certainly not in public. Of course, even if they don't talk about it, it doesn't mean they aren't thinking about it. More than anything, they are curious. They have the same feelings and sexual urges as anyone else, they just don't know how to channel them. I have a semi-prepared speech I give new girls I meet about sex being a natural, beautiful thing, and a physical expression of true love. It works. Usually.

A lot of outsiders think Chinese girls are 'easy.'
Is this true?
Sometimes.

As I've said before, it is impossible to label every Chinese person the same way. Like women of any other nationality, some will have sex with you the first time you meet. Most won't. In any case, there will almost always be some kind of agenda. Personally, I think this 'easy' reputation stems from a willingness to please and a sense of duty combined with a generally submissive nature. Another factor could be the preconceptions they have about Western culture. They think you expect them to fall into bed with you, and don't want you to be disappointed. It's often as simple as that.

Generally, Chinese women have their sexual awakening later than their western counterparts. Usually in their early-mid twenties. From then, for many it's like opening Pandora's Box. They take their time getting started, but when they do they discover a whole range of carnal delights and are eager to indulge fully and try almost anything. The fact that these things are considered 'forbidden' or at least frowned upon in the ultra-conservative Chinese society they were brought up in spurs them on more. But only behind closed doors. They enjoy pushing the boundaries, but Chinese women are very rarely overtly sexual in public.

Two words. Oral sex. Two more words. Give it. While most Chinese men expect no end of blow jobs, they are quite reticent about returning the favour. It's considered dirty and unhygienic. On the other hand, the majority of Western men love both giving and receiving. This is one benefit of having a more equal society, I suppose. You'll find lots of Chinese women fantasise about it, but few have ever actually experienced it. If you can do it properly, she will be yours forever.

The 'submissive' thing is interesting. Because of the perceived cultural requirements, you will find that a lot of Chinese women are naturally compliant and supine. Some, to the extreme. They like to be tied up and dominated. I once dated a woman from Tianjin who watched a lot of Japanese porn, which is obviously prevalent in Asia. Japanese porn can be pretty weird, with a lot of rape and incest scenarios. When we had sex, this woman would scream as if she were being murdered, and she loved it rough. I never found out whether she was into rough sex because she liked Japanese porn and thought that was the norm, or whether she liked Japanese porn because she was into rough sex.

Incidentally, this woman's name was Joy, and she was married to a guy in the Chinese navy. I met her when I had my teaching assistant (when you work with kids you are usually assigned an assistant to help bridge the language barrier) put up posters around the city advertising my one-on-one teaching services in an effort to make some extra money. She was a 'kept woman,' and her English level was already quite good. What she wanted to know about was things like politics and fashion. Things she couldn't learn about in the government-sanctioned text books. I think more than anything, she was just bored. She would come to my apartment for a couple of hours on weekends, and paid me a substantial fee, up front, for the privilege.

One day, after we'd been having lessons for a few weeks, she asked me how to use the word 'fuck' which she said she heard a lot in American TV shows.

I told her it was a very flexible word. You could say, "fuck you, fuck me, fuck this, fuck that, fuck Japan, or you could use it for emphasis, like 'I hate this fucking weather.'"

"So what would happen if I said, 'Fuck me?'"

"You know what would happen if you said that."

"So come on, fuck me."

And that was how it went. From that day on, we would just watch movies and have sex, and she still paid me. I even tried to give her money back, but she refused.

It was the best job I ever had.

I dated another Chinese woman who liked to call me 'Daddy' when we had sex. It was a turn-on at first. Until, one night, she asked 'Daddy' to read her a bedtime story while he fingered her. That was just too weird and I bailed.

Not every Chinese woman is submissive. With the elevated role of women in society and the creeping influence of feminism, an increasing number are being more sexually aggressive and like to take control in the bedroom. Let them, I say. Or take turns. Remember the vast majority of Chinese women, especially those below the age of 30 or so, are comparatively inexperienced and naive. For them, sex will be a journey of discovery, and you are the one in the control box.

You may be surprised at how attentive and willing to please your Chinese girlfriend will be, especially if you are more used to dating Western women. In a committed relationship, the woman will exist solely to pleasure her man. After an afternoon lovemaking session, it won't be unusual for her to suggest you take a nap while she cleans the apartment, washes your socks, then makes you a snack. It's endearing.

My first Chinese girlfriend, a 22-year old from Inner Mongolia who I met in Beijing, was very much into having sex in public places. That was bucking the trend, but I didn't know it at the time. It gave her a thrill, and given the choice she would always choose a park, a stairwell, a playground, or even a train over the sanctity and safety of a bedroom. We had sex on a bench in the Summer Palace, a popular tourist destination in Beijing, one afternoon. I'm pretty sure that if we'd been caught I would have been shot on sight, or at least deported. I think she got off on the danger of it all, or the possibility of being caught.

Interesting bit of background on the girl from Inner Mongolia; when she was growing up, her family was quite poor and struggled to pay for her schooling. A local businessman stepped up and offered to pay for her education, on the understanding that when she turned 16 she would enter into a sexual relationship with him. I don't know if the parents were aware of that part, but she certainly was. She felt she had little choice. If she wanted a better life, she was going to have to sleep with this guy. She eventually left her home town and went away to university, but had an agreement with him to go back every year and spend her birthday with him.

How did I find out about all this? Because when her birthday rolled around, after we'd been seeing each other for a few months, she was nowhere to be found. She wouldn't answer my calls, or text messages, or even my emails. Just when I was beginning to worry, she reappeared and confessed that she'd gone back to her home town to have a liaison with this guy.

When I found out, I hit the roof. Naturally. But what could I do? For all I knew, this might be common practice in the poorer provinces of China. I'd been in the country less than a year at that point.

Teddy Bears. In fact, stuffed animals of all description. Chinese girls, even when they surpass 30, absolutely love them. One girlfriend I had spent all her money on a massive four-foot cuddly penguin and insisted it 'slept' in the bed with us. I tried, for one night. Really I did. But I just found it too weird and banished the fucking thing to the wardrobe. A friend of mine refused to have sex with his Chinese girlfriend until she moved all 36 of her cuddly toys from her bed. She did so only under duress.

All this is to reinforce their desire to be looked after and cared for, just like a child. I imagine being a Chinese girl to be a bit like being Peter Pan. They never grow up.

When you enter into a sexual relationship with a Chinese woman, be aware that the responsibility for contraception rests squarely on your shoulders. Most Chinese women, especially those under 25 or so, have never even heard of the pill. This is one reason why there are so many abortions. In 2016 the US State Department claimed around 23 million are carried out each year in China. That's about 2625 an hour, far in excess of the official figure. Using comparative statistics, it's roughly 23 times more than the number carried out each year in the US. In reality, the true figure is likely to be even higher, especially if you take into account the recent surge in 'morning after' pills, which are readily available in chemists without prescription. The reason for this again lies in poor sex education and a general tendency to shy away from discussing sex.

STD's are rampant throughout China, which is one more reason to use condoms. AIDS and syphilis are the biggest worries, but the most widely-spread infection is Chlamydia and untreatable gonorrhoea is also on the rise. In fact, the problem is considered so serious in some quarters that the country has been described as being on the brink of catastrophe. Even in 1949, an estimated 10 million Chinese citizens carried some type of STD. Since then there has been a population explosion and a considerable rise in living standards, combined with increasing liberalization, Westernisation, and the so-called sexual revolution. The bottom line is that there are now more people having sex with more people in China than ever before, and most of them have no clue about contraception. Be part of the solution, not the problem.

Another stereotype among Western guys is that Chinese women, being generally smaller and more petite, have tighter vaginas.

Is this true?

I have to say that in my experience, and taking into consideration the western women I've slept with, there is an element of truth to it. One of my girlfriends was so tight, making love with her was like trying to force your finger into a clenched fist.

I will always remember the day an American colleague of mine knocked my door late one night on the hunt for some lubrication because he'd taken a girl home and their size difference was proving problematic. I told him to rub some butter on it and leave me alone.

Kidding.

Luckily for him, I had a few spare sachets of lube hanging around the apartment. I have never seen anyone so grateful.

Playing the Game

The so-called 'honeymoon period,' or the early stages of a relationship, should be plain sailing. It might be a little weird at times, like when your new girlfriend foregoes a bacon double cheeseburger in favour of a dead bird on a stick or some severed chicken's feet, but it's generally all fresh and exciting. However, Chinese women are complex creatures, and it takes time to get used to their cultural quirks and mannerisms. Personally, I find it all extremely interesting. When two people meet, especially those from different countries, it's like two worlds collide.

One thing to look out for is the sa jiao. There is no direct English translation, but it's basically when your grown-up girlfriend throws a temper tantrum and acts like a spoiled child, sometimes in public places. She will pout, stamp her feet, and talk in an annoying, whiny voice. Sometimes, she'll smack you across the face. At some point she will invariably say something like, "You don't love me. If you loved me, you'd buy me those shoes."

If you want my advice, just buy her the damn shoes and get on with your life.

The first time this happened to me, I had no idea what was going on and assumed the girl I was with was having some kind of mental breakdown. They do it because they think it makes them appear more feminine and childlike. Another side-effect of never growing up. It often manifests in something trivial like the inability to carry their own handbag, which can be annoying for Western guys who are used to dating women who value their independence more and wouldn't dream of handing over control of something as important as her handbag for even a split second. Chinese guys, however, supposedly find such helplessness attractive. Another of those weird little cultural differences.

Beware, this behaviour can also be one of those tests I mentioned, the objective being to see if a partner is willing to put the girl's needs above his own. Despite the inconvenience, the expense, and the general weirdness of it all, it's actually considered an honour if a girl sa jiao's to you. She will generally only do it to the two most important men in her life, the other being her father.

The deeper reason for all this is to enforce traditional gender roles. The man should be the provider; strong, resourceful, powerful, caring, domineering, and completely devoted to his partner. On the other hand, the girl should be weak, submissive, compliant and vulnerable. This, obviously, is completely at odds with western culture as most Western women would hate to be appear so needy.

Another interesting trait that maybe ties in with this is the attention-seeking. Chinese women will often engineer arguments with their other halves, often over something trivial. This is another test. They are gauging your reaction. If you have an argument and you are proved right, the worst thing you can do is throw it back at her at every given opportunity. You know you were right, and she knows you were right. Don't rub her nose in it, just let it lie and pretend that part of the conversation, the bit where you blew her argument out of the water, never happened. Again, this is linked to the whole 'saving face' thing. As a worthy partner, you have to do all you can to help preserve her 'face,' even at the expense of your own.

The golden rule here is that a Chinese woman is always right, even when she is wrong. If you forget everything else in this book, remember that one sentence. It will serve you well.

Something else they are fond of doing is feigning illness, or at least making the most out of minor ailments. Don't be surprised if your Chinese girlfriend demands to be taken to hospital if she catches a cold. Once there, it's almost guaranteed that she'll post pictures of an IV drip in her arm all over social media to elicit yet more attention.

This behaviour often rubs us up the wrong way because of the value we put on independence and self-sufficiency in Western culture. Having someone depend on us so much freaks us out. It's still your job to be the doting, attentive boyfriend. One thing you can be sure of is that if you perform this role well, she will reciprocate if or when you ever fall ill. Chinese women are generally more clingy than Western women. Some guys love it, others hate it. Whatever, if you want a Chinese girlfriend, you'd better just get used to it.

If you are thinking long-term, you will have to try a lot harder to keep things running smoothly. It won't happen naturally. No matter how attractive your new squeeze is, the chances are you'll run out of things to talk about quite quickly. Not because either one of you is not an interesting person. In fact, I would argue that the average Chinese person is far more interesting than the average Westerner simply because of the cultural diversity between our two cultures. The problem is the language barrier. No matter how well she learns

English, it will still be her second (sometimes third) language and she'll have problems expressing herself. Talking about food or catching a train, simple. But try discussing at length anything much deeper than that, like politics or the merits of Manchester United's back four, be prepared for a lot of blank looks.

Think about the process for a moment. If you ask her something, she first has to translate what you said into Chinese in her head, think of an answer, even though many of the words in her two vocabularies don't 'match,' then translate her answer into English and vocalize it. While all the time, you are staring at her expectantly.

Of course, to level the playing field you could try learning Mandarin (or Cantonese, depending on which language your girl speaks). But then you would be faced with the same problems from your side and despite what they like to tell you, both Mandarin and Cantonese are much, much harder to learn than English. You can learn the basics. A vocabulary of just 50 or 60 words will serve you extraordinarily well. But beyond that, things get very tricky.

Bear in mind, in all likelihood, she's been learning English since primary school, or even earlier, so she would have a significant advantage over you in that department. These days, more and more Western students are going to China to learn Chinese, so the language barrier presents less of a problem to them, but I always say you can either do that or work. You can't really do both to a high level, there just aren't enough hours in a day.

Without going too far into the psychology of it all, it is well documented that during the first few months, both parties in a relationship mirror the thoughts, emotions, and mannerisms of the other. We often do this subconsciously because we are so eager to please, and try to come across as the perfect partner. The result is that both halves present false representations of themselves, and it is this false representation that we fall in love with.

The problem is, after a while complacency sets in, and the mask slips. Too often, when people start showing their true personalities and dispositions, relationships disintegrate. That's when the honeymoon period is well and truly over and shit gets real.

If this happens, it might help if you try taking up a new hobby together, and don't sacrifice your social circle. Having one or two (preferably foreign) friends you can vent to and talk things over with can be a huge help. More often than not, any foreigner you meet in china will be going through similar things as you so you'll be able to compare notes and support each other.

When the cracks do start showing, she probably won't tell you what's bothering her or what you can do to improve the situation. She'll expect you to work it out yourself. Expect her to drop subtle hints, and then get even more inwardly angry when you don't pick up on them.

I always thought this was a bit unfair. When you are trying to assimilate into a different (and often bizarre) culture, and also have work pressures and daily life to contend with, sometimes the little things tend to pass you by. All you know is that your girlfriend is pissed off and you have no idea why. This is a reflection of Chinese society as a whole. They dislike confrontation, and will do anything to avoid it. Rather than address an issue, they prefer to brush it under the carpet.

One thing that keeps cropping up is a lack of self-confidence, which often manifests as jealousy bordering on paranoia. This stems mainly from the fact that while Chinese men are many things, monogamous is rarely one of them. Your Chinese girlfriend will want to know everything about you, which is sweet and endearing at first. This then extends to wanting to know your schedule, your movements, your habits, and where you are at any given time. Then, she'll keep notes, talk to your friends, and compare your stories to make sure you were telling the truth. If she even suspects you've been keeping secrets from her, she will either freak the fuck out or give you the silent treatment. Oh, and best not talk to, mention, or look at any other girls. Ever.

As a mixed race couple, you might face a certain degree of animosity from some factions. Many of the older generation still see foreigners as invaders and won't go out of their way to make you feel welcome. Rather than say something to you, they'll be far more likely to just stare at you. That takes some getting used to. Most Chinese guys also aren't overjoyed when they see foreigners dating Chinese girls, especially pretty ones. This is because of the gender imbalance. The last thing these guys want is more competition.

Temptation can also be a problem. If you are reasonably young and/or good-looking, it wouldn't be too much of an exaggeration to say that from time to time, women will throw themselves at you in China. The motivations obviously differ from person to person. One year, I was teaching a post-graduate course in Hunan province. These students were all in their mid-to-late twenties, and most had full-time jobs. After a class, one of the girls stayed behind to talk. They often do this. Some are curious about you and too shy to ask questions in class, others just want to practise their English.

"So what do I have to do to get a high mark in your class?" this girl asked, explaining that her employers had sent her to do a course she wasn't really interested in.

"It's pretty easy," I said. "You just have to come to class every week, or most weeks, and pass an oral exam at the end."

It's worth noting that most foreign teachers at Chinese universities aren't seen as 'real' teachers. They are more like status symbols used to attract students, and are therefore paid more and given less responsibility than their Chinese counterparts. A lot of what foreign teachers do amounts to ticking boxes. None of this sits well with Chinese teachers, who don't often try very hard to disguise their contempt.

What the girl said next shocked me to the core. "Well, I don't have time to come to class every week. So how about we make love instead, and you give me a good mark?"

I wasn't sure I heard correctly, or I thought maybe we were having some kind of communication breakdown. "Do you know what you're saying?" I asked.

"Yes."

"I'm not sure that would be legal, or moral."

"Just one-time sex. I won't tell anybody if you won't. I know men like sex. This is just an easy way for us both to get what we want. You can think about it."

I did think about it. A lot. To her next class, this girl wore the shortest skirt I've ever seen and sat right at the front, practically waving her legs in my face. She acquired my phone number from the class monitor and started texting me all the time. Usually, whenever she was out clubbing and had a few drinks inside her. A few weeks later, she collared me after class again. "Did you think about my suggestion?" she asked with a smirk.

I brushed her off, but could feel my defences weakening. What would be the harm? I had a suspicion this kind of thing happened a lot in China, and quite possibly elsewhere. I couldn't really blame her. She was just playing the cards she'd been dealt and using every means at her disposal to get ahead. The Chinese are nothing if not resourceful. In the end, I slept with her to get rid of her.

But that wasn't quite the end of the matter.

After the 'one-time sex,' she started texting and calling me all the time and turning up at my door unannounced. Then she started talking about buying a house in France and sending me links to estate agents. I began to worry about what she might do next. I ignored her as much as I could, so then she hit me with a sucker punch and told me she was pregnant and wanted to start planning the wedding as soon as possible. The one and only time we'd had sex I'd used a condom, but I acknowledged that it was possible she might still have got pregnant, especially given the inferior quality of Chinese condoms. Extraordinarily unlikely, but possible. In any case, I called her bluff and told her that I would be glad to start planning the wedding and looking for the house in France, just as long as a paternity test confirmed the baby was mine. She backed off after that.

Several other Chinese women I've known have played the 'I'm pregnant' card over the years. They have ways and means of getting what they want, and can be very coercive, even manipulative, at times. Others just like creating drama. Those damned weird character tests. They want to see if you'll accept responsibility, and therefore be a worthy partner or not. If that's the case, I guess I failed every test because on each occasion I've run a mile.

The Long Haul

As I've said before, there is a general feeling among a lot of Chinese women that foreigners are for fun, and Chinese guys are for something more serious. This notion is partly fuelled by the fact that most foreigners don't settle in China for long. Usually only a year or two. Sometimes, a lot less. That said, I know a few foreigners who have married Chinese women. The American guy who knocked my door one night looking for lube? Yep, he ended up marrying that girl and taking her back to America with him where they bought a book store and lived happily ever after. Up to now, anyway.

If you plan on getting hitched to a Chinese girl, perhaps the biggest hurdle you will face is convincing her parents that letting her marry you is a good idea. They'll want assurances, and will probably demand you at least own your own house and car. And no, renting doesn't count. Also, know that in Chinese culture, the husband hands over the purse strings to the wife. In effect, this means he signs over full control of his savings, assets and bank accounts. Taking care of business behind the scenes, i.e. Paying bills, etc, is traditionally seen as the woman's role. If you want a happy, stress-free life, don't fight it. Just trust in your partner. Chances are she has your best interests at heart and every financial decision she makes will benefit you in the long run.

Parents rely on their offspring to look after them in their old age, both financially and physically, and they don't want to see their meal ticket decamp to a different country. You might be asked to pay an endowment, especially if your wife-to-be is from a rural area. In effect, the parents put their daughter up for tender, and 'sell' her to the highest bidder. How much you'll be expected to pay for her hand in marriage varies widely and there are no hard and fast rules. A recent article in the South China Post claimed that a typical Beijinger would have to part with around 200,000 RMB (£22,650) as well as own an apartment in the city. The article went on to state that in line with the country's financial boom, this represents a twenty-fold rise in just four years, and that it generally costs more in the north than it does in the south.

You might find it unbelievable in this day and age, but arranged marriages are still a thing in China. When people of both sexes reach their mid-twenties their families will start to pile the pressure on, and if their offspring aren't yet in a serious relationship, the parents will often do a bit of matchmaking. Obviously, they have vastly different agendas to their kids, and veer sharply towards setting them up with people who have an abundance of cash. This might seem a little mercenary, and it is. The better life their kids have, the better life the parents will have when they reach old age. They view their children as something akin to an insurance policy, and little things like love and compatibility rarely enter the equation. These are invariably perfunctory marriages of convenience with very little in the way of passion or excitement. There is a general idea that these things quickly wear off, anyway. Hence, there are a lot of unsatisfied spouses in China, and the divorce rate is rocketing as more and more people work out that it doesn't have to be that way.

Time for a story. One afternoon, a student of mine asked if we could go somewhere quiet for a chat. The first thing she did was thank me for the lessons, and said she owed me a proper goodbye. I wasn't expecting that as we were midway through the semester, and thought she might be suffering a crisis of confidence or something. It turned out to be worse than that. She asked me how she could learn German in two weeks. I told her that was pretty much an impossible task and asked why she wanted to know. She explained that her parents had arranged for her to go to Germany to marry a Chinese doctor who'd moved there. A friend of the family.

I asked if she'd ever met her future husband, and she said no but they'd talked on Skype once. He had kind eyes. The worst thing for her, apart from the all the upheaval, stress and uncertainty, was being forced to leave the boyfriend she'd been with for three years who'd been deemed 'unsuitable' by her parents. I told her to run away to another city with him, but she didn't want to go against her parent's wishes. Being an only child, she carried the weight of a family's hopes on her shoulders. After that day, I never saw her again, and can only assume she's shacked up with a doctor in Germany. I hope she's happy.

Some Chinese people try to cover all bases. I once knew a woman in Shanghai who was the mistress of a rich businessman. He had been forced into an arranged marriage so kept this woman as a bit on the side. He paid for her apartment in a plush part of the city, and even gave her a monthly stipend. They weren't exclusive, and he didn't mind her dating other guys, just as long as she was 'available' a couple of nights a week. In Chinese they call the third person in a relationship 'xiao san,' or 'Little Three.'

It's also not unusual for people to have long-term boyfriends or girlfriends in their home town and then date other people when they move to other cities for work, much like Jody did with me in Changsha, if you remember. They don't usually see anything immoral or duplicitous about it. It's considered practical, and an accepted (though rarely discussed) part of the culture. More often than not, when they've made some money they return to the provinces and settle down with the childhood sweetheart.

Interestingly, you will find a lot of Chinese women eventually marry ex-schoolmates. This is partly due to an old Chinese legend which decrees that couples destined to marry are tied together during their childhood by invisible red strings (yeah, I know, if they're invisible, how do they know the strings are red?). As they grow up, the strings binding them together become shorter and shorter until it is time for them to marry. Nothing can sever the strings. Not distance, changing circumstances, or the love of another. If you didn't know, red is considered an especially auspicious and lucky colour in China. Traditionally, the bride will wear a red dress on her wedding day and accept gifts in the form of red envelopes stuffed with cash.

As you may have gathered by now, Chinese women love drama. One way they express this is by going in search of a last fling before they get married and settle down. A couple of years ago, I added a hot Chinese girl who popped up in my Facebook feed. She lived in a city in Hunan province where I taught for a year and we had a few mutual friends. We made small talk for a while, then moved over to WeChat which made things easier for her. I knew she had a long-term boyfriend from the start, but that didn't make her any less desirable. We grew quite close, though I always knew she was out of reach. Until one day she announced she was coming to the UK to do an English course.

I offered to meet her and show her around, and she accepted. We had dinner together, then I took her to a Wetherspoons (a pub chain) in Nottingham for a drink. At the end of the evening I left to make my way back to my hotel, but she insisted on coming with me. Then ensued one of the hottest nights of sex I've ever had. We must have done it five or six times, in every position imaginable, until the sun came up to find us tangled up in a sweaty heap on the bed. She explained that she was getting married soon. Ouch. And that she wanted a 'wild night' before tying the knot. I think we achieved that much, but it came at a hefty price.

In the morning we said our goodbye's, and not long after she returned to China. I tried to send her a message to see if she arrived in one piece only to find that she'd blocked me on both WeChat and Facebook. I told you how ruthless Chinese women can be. Believe it.

In China, if a woman reaches the age of 30 and is still unmarried, she will be considered a 'leftover woman.' This is the equivalent of 'being left on the shelf,' but in China the connotations are a lot more serious. To be single at 30 in the west is perfectly acceptable, but to be single at 30 in the east it is considered a source of shame. Not just for you, but more importantly for your family. There is a derogatory term, sheng nu, used to describe leftover women in certain circles, as if being called 'leftover' wasn't insulting enough. You may also hear them referred to as 3S, which stands for 'Single, Seventies (as in born in the 1970's) and Stuck.'

What does this mean for foreign men with a more flexible set of standards?

It means single women approaching the watershed age of 30, mortally afraid of becoming 'leftover women,' relax their standards significantly. In fact, if you are of a similar age or older, and foreign, they would absolutely love to go out with you. The NBS (National Bureau of Statistics) estimate that approximately 1 in 5 women in China fall into this category. In numerical terms, that would be somewhere in the region of 120 million.

Something else that has a significant social stigma attached to it in China is being a single mother, especially if you have a son. In fact, there are very few. This is because most single mothers would prefer to marry someone, anyone, than be alone. Desperation isn't attractive, but it certainly increases your chances of getting laid.

Unlike in Western culture, where people don't generally care too much about their lover's past, if you are a Chinese divorcee the overwhelming feeling is that you must be some kind of failure. However, with the marriage rate falling and the divorce rate climbing, this attitude is certain to change in the not-too-distant future. If I had the time and resources, I'd retrain as a divorce lawyer and move back to China. I'd make a killing.

Paying for It

Of course, like most places in Asia, or indeed, the world, if all else fails you can just pay for sex. Prostitution is technically illegal in China, but it's much more common than you would probably think, especially in light of the financial boom. Confession time: Earlier in this book when I estimated I had slept with up to 50 Chinese women, if I factor in the ones I've paid for, that figure would easily be over 100.

This is how it generally works: Girls simply move to a city nobody knows them, sign up with a brothel, and tell their families they work in an office or something. In the brothels they are safe and protected, and can earn much more than they can working a conventional job, and in a much shorter time-frame. Most do it for a year or two to make some capital, then they start a business, go to university, or use the money to buy a house. Some students do it during the holidays to help pay their tuition fees. Heck, you see cars kerb-crawling outside universities all the time. These girls are young, beautiful, and often have very little money so they are usually open to suggestions. I'm not saying it's right, I'm just telling you what happens.

Obviously, it's all done on the quiet and different cities have different ways of shielding the practice. In the large international hotels in the major cities, they slide business cards with a phone number under your hotel door after bribing the hotel staff to let them in. You just ring them and tell them the name of your hotel and your room number. They probably won't speak English, but they'll understand that much.

Down south, they masquerade as hairdressing salons. These you can spot because nobody is actually getting their hair cut, there are just half a dozen young women sitting around in skimpy clothes playing on their phones. In Hong Kong, pimps will walk up to you in the street and offer to find you a 'date,' while in Tianjin and many other cities, they use public bath houses as fronts. You go for a sauna, or a swim, and then are ushered upstairs.

Another place you can often pay for sex are KTV (karaoke) bars. These are everywhere in China. Inside, many places hire hostesses in the same way as other places hire the aforementioned bar girls. Their job is to ply you with drink, sing for you, and, very often, accompany you back to your hotel. These generally work out more expensive because they pray on drunk people.

Weirdly, in my experience, establishments that advertise themselves as massage parlours usually tend to be legitimate. They really do want to give you a Chinese massage. Most will, however, offer a 'happy ending' for an increased fee. Once, I paid an exceptionally hot girl more if she did it topless. She readily agreed, but drew the line at actually having sex with me.

Apparently, a lot of massage parlours, KTV joints and brothels are owned by ex-policemen and soldiers, who use their connections, relationships and influence (collectively known as 'guanxi') to keep the places open and avoid being shut down. That's how things work in China. If a competing brothel was opened by someone who didn't have the right connections, it wouldn't last five minutes. The same can be said for any kind of business.

Prices can vary greatly, depending on the location, the establishment, and the girl. The lowest I ever paid was 100 RMB (£11) and the highest around 600 (£66). Be prepared to pay more during public holidays, especially Spring Festival. Some places will charge you more than they would charge a local guy. This happens a lot. Not just in brothels, but small shops, too. They have one pay scale for locals, and a different one for foreigners. While we might be insulted by the practice – it's illegal in most Western countries – it's common in China, the logic being that westerners have more money so can afford to pay more.

You might find some places flat-out refuse to let you in if you're foreign. This, of course, is blatantly racist, but what are you going to do? Go to the police and complain that a brothel you visited was mean to you? You can try bribing the guy on the door with a hundred RMB bill or two, or offering to pay the girl more money, but you'd probably be better off just taking it on the chin and moving on to the next place. You usually find them in clusters, anyway. If they don't want your money, give it to someone else. Amusingly, in an attempt to soften the blow, they sometimes tell you that they won't cater for your needs because your dick is too big for them.

There is generally less of a stigma attached to using these places than there is in the West. Lots of more affluent Chinese men simply incorporate it into their routine in the same way they would a foot massage. In Hunan province where I lived for several years, pink lighting is always a dead giveaway, but don't forget to look up.

Many of these premises are not situated on street level, but in the upper floors of apartment blocks. You will invariably find them in the suburbs, away from the city centres, and quite often in student areas. Female students want to make money, and male students want sex.

You usually walk into a sitting room and take a seat on a couch, surrounded by women in short skirts. Either that, or you sit there whilst a procession of beautiful young girls come in and parade in front of you, each better looking than the last. I suppose, even considering the difference in perceived beauty between east and west, in those situations unattractive girls would tend to get overlooked in favour of hotter ones and soon drift out of the profession. Even poorly-paid factory or office work is better than no work at all.

You make your choice, and the girl will take you to a private room. This might be in the back somewhere or an entirely different building. There, you will both take a shower, and she'll probably give you a rudimentary massage. This is all a precursor to sex. It's very safe and clean, and the girls always use condoms.

The details vary from place to place and girl to girl. One of my favourite girls, who I met dozens of times and built up a good working relationship with, used 'fire and ice' treatment, whereby she would alternate sucking my dick with ice cubes and hot water in her mouth.

As ever, though, take precautions and always be aware of your surroundings. There's a scam whereby dumb foreigners are led into a room under the pretence of meeting a prostitute, only to be fake-arrested by a couple of goons pretending to be policemen. Of course, they offer to drop all the charges against you if you pay them a large sum of money. I've heard other stories about foreigners being robbed when they are distracted or at their most vulnerable. For this reason, I rarely take out more money than I need and always leave my bank cards at home.

I don't see it as taking advantage of anybody. I'm sure it happens, but I've never talked to a prostitute who was kidnapped and sold into the sex trade, like the scaremongering Western media would have you believe. All the girls I met went into it with their eyes open, and for the simple fact that they can make more money sleeping with people than they can doing menial jobs. For me, it's just like using any other kind of service. I'm contributing to the economy.

I take the Charlie Sheen attitude toward prostitutes. I don't pay them to have sex with me, I pay them to leave. I'm not going to lie about it. Being in any kind of relationship is exhausting, but because of all the things I've talked about in this book, dating Chinese women is even more debilitating and emotionally draining than dating women from your own culture. Sometimes I just want to fuck someone and walk away, and I don't mind paying for the privilege.

Top Tips for Dating Chinese Women

1: To make a good impression, always be polite and respectful - open doors, pull her chair out for her in the restaurant, let her choose from the menu first, etc.

2: Be attentive, and ask her questions about herself. Even if you aren't generally interested, fake it.

3: Dress smartly and look presentable.

4: Wear aftershave

5: Steer the conversation towards your assets - your house, car, earnings, savings, etc.

6: Know the basics about Chinese culture, and learn at least a few words or phrases to show you are willing to make the effort.

7: Be positive, and never openly criticize your family. The family unit is very important in Chinese culture, don't disrespect it.

8: Don't put pressure on her. Let things move at her pace, which will probably be a lot slower than you are used to.

9: That said, remember the onus is on you to take the lead. Expect to be forced to break through a wall of token resistance.

10: Impress her. She likely has many potential suitors. Stand out from the crowd. Luckily for you, being a foreigner, that part is effectively done for you.

11: Try to display some of the qualities she likes; kindness, responsibility, and a good sense of humour are top of the list.

**Bonus Content:
Yellow Fever: Love & Sex in China
Extract**

Mid-autumn festival rolled around again. This is the time of year when everyone in China exchanges mooncakes. Mooncakes are round pastries meant to represent the moon, and look very appetising. But aren't usually that great, if truth be told. They look like they should taste sweet, but they don't. If you're lucky yours might have some bits of dried fruit inside, otherwise you'll find red bean paste or maybe salted egg.

This particular festival I received a text from Jane, another one of my old students from HMMC. I was surprised, because although we'd a good relationship when I'd taught her, we hadn't talked much since. She belatedly welcomed me back to China, and suggested we go out for dinner.

"When?"

"Now."

I didn't have any other plans that evening, so I agreed. A couple of hours later she arrived wearing a short sexy green dress, and we had an unremarkable meal at a nearby restaurant. Afterwards, I walked her to the bus stop. When we got there she said she'd just missed her last bus home, and would I mind if she spent the night at my place. Of course I didn't mind, she was beautiful. But I was pretty sure the last bus hadn't come yet. Evidently, so were the small crowd of people standing there waiting for it.

To make absolutely certain we weren't operating at cross purposes, I offered to pay for a taxi. Jane declined, saying she didn't want to waste my money. By now, I knew the drill. If she had really wanted to leave, she would have. In fact, she would have left long ago. According to Dora's logic, if she didn't want to be there she wouldn't have come in the first place. The predicament we found ourselves in had been carefully engineered. Just like it had been countless times before; Alice, Dora, Cherry Pie, Lily, I felt a bit manipulated. But at the same time, that rush was still there. The excitement of potentially sleeping with a different girl. A bit of strange.

Back at my apartment Jane announced she was tired and was going straight to bed, despite it not even being ten pm. I guess she knew I wouldn't pass up the chance to accompany her. She also decided her short sexy green dress wasn't adequate sleep wear, and got changed into one of my old t-shirts. We got in bed, and immediately started kissing and fondling. I soon reclaimed my tshirt, and was in the act of relieving her of her underwear when there was a knock at the door.

I froze. I wasn't expecting anyone. I decided to ignore it and carried on with the task at hand.

Another knock, louder this time.

Shit.

I pulled on my jeans and went to the door, fully expecting one of my American colleagues who lived upstairs to be on the hunt for cigarettes or something. But when I opened it, I was amazed to find Ebony, my ex from Xiangtan, standing there holding a shopping bag.

"Happy mid-autumn festival," she said.

"What are you doing here?"

"I missed you, and didn't want you to be alone on a Chinese special day, so I come see you."

"Ebony... we broke up. Remember?" Not only that, but we hadn't even talked for several months. I remember telling her where my new job was, but I didn't tell her where on the campus I lived. I hadn't known myself until I arrived. Evidently, she'd gone to the university and just walked around asking people where I was until she found me. This was a bolt from the blue, and I don't like surprises.

"I brought you beer and mooncakes."

Her face was wet with tears. Damn it. "You can't come in, Ebony."

"Why?"

Right there was my chance to nip things in the bud. Just explain that I had moved on, there was someone else in the apartment, and it wasn't a good idea that they meet. She would have been pissed off, but would've understood. Then I could have gone back and had my wicked way with Jane with an almost-clear conscience.

But I didn't do that. Instead, I lied through my teeth. I like to think it was another Happy Lie, because it averted a potentially awkward situation. But the truth is, I bottled it. I didn't want the confrontation. So I made up something about the apartment being decorated, and led Ebony down the stairs. I had no idea where to go, I just needed to buy some time to think. What the fuck was I going to do? It was too late for either girl to go home, there was no chance of them staying in the same place, and I really wanted to bang Jane.

I took Ebony to a nearby outdoor barbecue place, ordered her some food, and sent Jane a message saying my friend's dog had run away and I was out helping him look for it. Second Happy Lie of the evening. Second Happy Lie in about six minutes, to be precise.

Then I had an idea. I called one of my American colleagues and asked if there was a hotel on campus. Of course there was. It turned out there was a hotel directly across the street from where I lived. I don't know how I hadn't noticed it before.

Being a festival weekend, there was only one room left. The penthouse suit, which took up most of the top floor and was about five times the price of an ordinary room. I told Ebony I would pay for it, and take her to breakfast in the morning, but I couldn't stay the night with her. She started crying, and I wilted under the pressure. Naturally, we got down to business quite quickly, and I fucked her over the balcony as cars and people went past on the road below. In fact, if Jane had looked out of the living room window of my apartment, she might even have seen me.

The minute Ebony's head hit the pillow she was asleep, and I immediately let myself out of the hotel room and ran across the road back to my apartment. I'd been gone an hour or two by this point, and Jane was justifiably put out by my sudden disappearance. It took all my skills of persuasion to advance things to the point they were at before Ebony had appeared. This time, I actually penetrated her. I was inside her, missionary position, and lifting her knees to make entry easier. I was about half way in when there was another knock at the door.

Not now. Please, not now.

I tried to ignore it, but I felt Jane's body tense up underneath me. Then came another succession of knocks, getting progressively louder and more angry-sounding.

I withdrew, mumbled an apology, put my jeans back on, shut the bedroom door behind me and flung open the front door. I knew it would be Ebony, but I didn't know how pissed off she would be. She threw herself at me, punching, kicking and screaming. It was all I could do to wrestle her out of my apartment. I blamed the phantom decorators again, but I'm pretty sure Happy Lie Numero Uno was wearing a bit thin by that point. I eventually managed to persuade her to go back to the hotel, and because I was so afraid she would go full nuclear again if I left her alone, I stayed with her.

First thing in the morning I gave Ebony some money and put her on a bus, then legged it back to my place. I was hoping to have another crack at Jane and maybe finish what we had started (twice), or at least have breakfast with her. But she was gone. The bed was made and all my belongings were still there, which was a huge bonus. We didn't talk again for a couple of years, and when we did she was understandably frosty. Another Chinese girl who will never forgive me for trying to do the right thing.

About the Author

Alex Coverdale a London-based journalist, editor and dark fiction writer. He uses a pseudonym, rather than his real name, to protect the guilty as well as the innocent. And also because he doesn't want his friends and family to know what he really gets up to when he travels. He has spent over a decade living and working in China and has visited over 20 other countries, the experiences shaping him both as a person and as a writer. His work has appeared in almost 100 publications worldwide, and he is the author of several #1 Amazon bestsellers.

For more information, and to keep up with new adventures, please visit his website:

https://coverdalewrites.wordpress.com/

Or follow him on Facebook.

https://www.facebook.com/Alex.Coverdale.27

Books by Alex Coverdale:

Dating Chinese Women: Tips, Tricks & Techniques
Thailand: 27 Days of Sin

This is China: Misadventures in the Middle Kingdom series

Part 1: The North
Part 2: Hunan Province
Part 3: The Wilderness Years
Part 4: The Return

Praise for the Author:

"The writing felt very personal and real. At the end of the book I felt like I had lived another life...an interesting one to boot."

"The author was the forbidden fruit to Chinese girls and in describing his experiences he gives some insights into the Chinese mindset. And this is the most valuable part of his book."

"Highly recommended for those interested in the expat teacher lifestyle in China."

"A great insight to how another part of the world works."

This is China: Misadventures in the Middle Kingdom

Part 1: The North

(Exclusive Extract)

Upping sticks and moving to China was a big step. A big step I didn't want to take by myself. I thought I would be a lot happier if someone came with me, so I asked around. Most of my university friends had moved into marketing or telesales by then, or even worse, ended up as office drones at some bank or building society. Nobody was interested in embarking on an adventure in the Far East.

Except Kim.

Kim, a slightly dorky, doe-eyed middle-class English girl, absolutely loved the idea. Over drinks one night she asked some questions about the job and my contacts, and after a bit of gentle persuading decided to apply herself. The school I was hooked up with needed a whole bunch of English teachers, not just one.

The moment I mentioned China to Kim, I regretted it. She had a reputation as a bit of a drama queen. On a student night at a club once there'd been a group of guys dressed up as Smurfs. They all wore loincloths, white hats, and painted themselves blue. In a drunken stupor, one of them shoved his hand up Kim's skirt. She freaked out and called the police. When they arrived they asked Kim what the guy who'd assaulted her looked like. She replied, "He looked like a Smurf."

Naturally, when the police tried to investigate the matter further they found that there were about nineteen guys dressed as Smurfs in the club that night, and by then they were all falling over drunk. I would have paid good money to see that identity parade.

Kim and I had dated a few times, and usually ended up in bed together, but our thing, whatever it was, had long-since fizzled out and she was now involved with a posh bloke called Mark. It was going to be awkward.

In the build-up to my departure date, I was a bag of nerves. The closer it got, the more terrified I became. There was an element of excitement but yeah, mostly blind terror. I was stepping into the unknown and had no idea what to expect. I felt like I was being swept away on a tide. Things had spiralled way out of control. Kim felt much the same, so we decided to hold a DYING IN CHINA party before we went to say goodbye to everyone. This was hastily changed to a HOPING TO SURVIVE CHINA at the request of her boyfriend Mark.

There was a lot of paperwork involved. First I had to apply for and get the job, which bizarrely turned out to be the easiest part of the whole process. You just had to be a native English speaker with a degree in any subject and no criminal record. There were no background checks. Not that I know of, anyway. It was simply a case of them asking me whether I had any criminal convictions, and me replying in the negative. Once an agreement had been reached, I signed a contract and waited for the official invitation letter from my prospective employer to arrive, which I could then use to get a tourist visa (known as an L visa) which granted me initial entry into the country. At a later date the L visa could be converted to a multiple-entry Z visa, which doubles as a work and residency permit. I also had to pass a medical examination, book flights, do some research, and make various other arrangements. It was during this period that I had my first brush with Chinese bureaucracy. Unfortunately, it wouldn't be my last.

Shortly after I'd submitted my visa application, the phone rang. On the other end was a very pleasant sounding lady speaking with a choppy Chinese accent who said she was from the Chinese embassy in London, where my visa application was being processed.

"I want to tell you we received your application."

"Good."

"Not good. Problem."

"Oh? What's that?"

"I sorry to tell you, we unable to grant you visa to come China."

"What? Why is that?"

"Application say you are journalist. Journalist need special permission from Chinese government to come China. You have special permission from Chinese government?"

"No."

"Then no come China."

I knew Chinese authorities are generally suspicious of overseas journalists. They kept their own journalists on a tight leash, but had no such jurisdiction over foreigners and this being in the run-up to the 2008 Olympics in Beijing they were being especially vigilant, something that had never even occurred to me. In the face of such officious-sounding bullshit, I began to panic. "But I have a job to go to in China, and I've already paid for my flights. The tickets are non-refundable. Is there anything I can do?" I asked, more out of hope than expectation.

"Yes. You do new application. Only this time, say you do different job. No journalist. Understand?"

No, I didn't understand at all. I thought I did, but I must surely be mistaken. "You want me to... lie?"

"No lie. Just say you do different job. No journalist."

"But I don't do a different job. So it's lying."

"No lying."

"But wouldn't it be illegal?"

"Is okay."

"Well, if you say so." I still wasn't convinced, but didn't think I had much choice other than to do what this lady was suggesting. Even then, there was another problem. "If I submit another visa application, there won't be enough time," I protested. "It would take too long to process. I'd have to get new forms, fill them in, and post them back to you. It would require a few days. Plus, you have my passport, so I can't even do that until you send my passport back."

"Okay, first option is we keep passport and you come London, fill out form, submit same day. Pay express fee."

"Is there a second option?"

"Of course. You just ask friend to do it for you."

"What friend?"

"Any friend. You have friend in London?"

"Yes, but won't the application need my signature on it?"

"Your friend can do it."

Wow. For a country evidently so pre-occupied with following rules and regulations, China seemed to be surprisingly lax in other areas. It didn't make much sense, but I wasn't going to question it. I just did what they said and had a friend go to the embassy, fill out another application on my behalf, and forge my signature. Job done. Days later my passport was returned to me boasting a Chinese L visa and couple of weeks after that, I was on a plane to Beijing.

Thank you for reading this book! Please spread the word and consider leaving an honest review on Amazon or Goodreads.

Created with Writer2ePub
by Luca Calcinai

Printed in Great Britain
by Amazon